The Fall of Sleep

The Fall of Sleep

JEAN-LUC NANCY

TRANSLATED BY CHARLOTTE MANDELL

FORDHAM UNIVERSITY PRESS ✦ *New York*

This work was originally published in French as Jean-Luc Nancy, *Tombe de sommeil* © 2007 Éditions Galilée, Paris.

Copyright © 2009 Fordham University Press

All rights reserved. No part of this publication may be reproduced, stored in a retrieval system, or transmitted in any form or by any means—electronic, mechanical, photocopy, recording, or any other—except for brief quotations in printed reviews, without the prior permission of the publisher.

This work has been published with the assistance of the French Ministry of Culture—National Center for the Book.

Ouvrage publié avec le concours du Ministère français chargé de la culture—Centre National du Livre.

Library of Congress Cataloging-in-Publication Data

Nancy, Jean-Luc.
[Tombe de sommeil. English]
The fall of sleep / Jean-Luc Nancy ; translated by Charlotte Mandell.
 p. cm.
Includes bibliographical references.
ISBN 978-0-8232-3117-1 (cloth : alk. paper)
ISBN 978-0-8232-3118-8 (pbk. : alk. paper)
1. Sleep—Psychological aspects. I. Title.
BF1071.N3513 2009
154.6—dc22
                    2009020853

Printed in the United States of America
11 10 09   5 4 3 2 1
First edition

Now comes the peal of the distant clock, with fainter and fainter strokes as you plunge further into the wilderness of sleep. It is the knell of a temporary death. Your spirit has departed, and strays like a free citizen, among the people of a shadowy world.
    —Nathaniel Hawthorne, "The Haunted Mind,"
      in *Twice Told Tales*

Contents

Translator's Note ✦ *ix*

1. To Fall Asleep ✦ *1*
2. I'm Falling Asleep ✦ *5*
3. Self from Absence to Self ✦ *11*
4. Equal World ✦ *17*
5. "To sleep, perchance to dream, ay, there's the rub . . ." ✦ *23*
6. Lullaby ✦ *29*
7. The Soul That Never Sleeps ✦ *35*
8. The Knell [*Glas*] of a Temporary Death ✦ *41*
9. The Blind Task of Sleep ✦ *47*

Notes ✦ *49*

Translator's Note

The titles of Jean-Luc Nancy's books, like those of Maurice Blanchot, pose interesting challenges to the translator, fraught as they are with puns and alternative meanings. The original French title of this book is *Tombe de Sommeil*, which means "Tomb of Sleep." Or "tombstone of sleep" or "monument of sleep." "Tomb," however, and its relatives, does not have the same resonance for English-speaking readers as it does for French readers, who feel its connection to the verb *tomber*, "to fall." Readers of Derrida's *Glas* will be reminded of his glosses on the word *tombe* and the links to tomb/tombstone/*chute*("fall")/*tomber*.

In French, *tomber de sommeil* (literally, "to fall from sleep") is an idiomatic expression meaning "to drop from exhaustion, to be falling asleep on one's feet." Since falling is an essential trope throughout this book, some titles I considered were *Sleepfall*, *Falling Asleep*, *Lullaby* . . . The present title was finally settled on after consultation with the author, for whose advice I am grateful.

I would like to thank my editor, Helen Tartar, for giving me the opportunity to translate this lovely meditation on sleep and my husband, Robert Kelly, for his editorial advice.

Charlotte Mandell
Annandale-on-Hudson

The Fall of Sleep

1

To Fall Asleep

I'm falling asleep.[1] I'm falling into sleep and I'm falling there by the power of sleep. Just as I fall asleep from exhaustion. Just as I drop from boredom.[2] As I fall on hard times. As I fall, in general. Sleep sums up all these falls, it gathers them together. Sleep is proclaimed and symbolized by the sign of the fall, the more or less swift descent or sagging, faintness.

To these we can add: how I'm fainting from pleasure, or from pain. This fall, in its turn, in one or another of its versions, mingles with the others. When I fall into sleep, when I sink, everything has become indistinct, pleasure and pain, pleasure itself and its own pain, pain itself and its own pleasure. One passing into the other produces exhaustion, lassitude, boredom, lethargy, untying, unmooring. The boat gently leaves its moorings, and drifts.

The pain of pleasure comes when pleasure can no longer bear itself. It's when it gives itself up and stops allowing itself solely to enjoy [*jouir*]. Exhausted lovers fall asleep. The pleasure of pain is when pain insists, not without perversity, that it should be sustained, and savored even, while it grows increasingly inflamed. It's when it revels, if only in its own lament. It doesn't just let itself struggle and protest against the pain; by itself it agrees to fall asleep in a way—in the sense that we say "put the pain to sleep"—even if it means enduring a dreadful reawakening.

In any case, faintness and falling consist in not allowing a state to persist with the tension natural to it (a state of tension, then, that is not a "state"). With its tension and its intention slackening, giving up: activity into fatigue, interest into boredom, hope or confidence into distress, pleasure into displeasure, rejection of pain into morose delectation of it. Keenness becomes dull, momentum is lost, an alertness falls asleep.

*　*　*

An alertness falls asleep: that is how from all quarters we are led or led back toward the motif of sleep as soon as any kind of faintness is expressed, as soon as any renunciation appears, an abandon, a decrease or a retreat of intentionality under any of its forms.

An alertness falls asleep, for, by definition, it is only alertness that can fall asleep. Wakefulness alone can give way to sleep, and wakefulness preserved stems from sleep refused, sleepiness refused. The sentinel must struggle against sleep, as does Aeschylus's watchman on the roof, as Christ's companions forget to do. Whoever relinquishes vigilance relinquishes attention and intention, every kind

TO FALL ASLEEP

of tension and anticipation; he enters into the unraveling of plans and aims, of expectations and calculations. It is this loosening that gathers together—actually or symbolically—the fall into sleep. This fall is the fall of a tension, it is a relaxation that is not content with an inferior, limited degree of tension but that sinks down toward an infinitesimal proximity to degree zero: until that underlying closeness to simple inertia that we know in the bodies of sleeping infants, which we sometimes recognize when on the edge of sleep we can feel that we are beginning to stop feeling the basic energy of our bodies. We feel the suspense of feeling. We feel ourselves falling, we feel the fall.

* * *

We fall from sleep into sleep: sleep is itself a force that precedes itself and that carries its power forward into its action. If I'm falling asleep, it's because already sleep has begun to take control of me and invade me even before I sleep, before I've begun to fall. We say that sleep conquers us: it gains on us, it extends its hold and its shadow with the discretion and constancy that are those of the evening, of dust, of age.

This antecedence of sleep can be prolonged indefinitely. Thus, ancient monuments do not, strictly speaking, sleep, but they are plunged into somnolence, into a drowsiness that stems from their abandonment, the prime example of which has long been the Sphinx of Gizeh, along with the statues on Easter Island. Neither our curiosity nor our admiration can awaken the gods, the princes, the conquerors, or the crowds made to labor or pray for their celebrations.

THE FALL OF SLEEP

As we say in French, these monuments are *désaffectés*, disused, deconsecrated: they are emptied of their responsibilities and, with them, emptied of the affects they once roused. The pyramids of Egypt or Mexico, imperial or royal palaces, temples and cathedrals keep being conquered by a sleep that can neither put them completely to sleep nor consign them to a free existence as ruins that could have another life, a metamorphosis, even a metempsychosis—as happens when the ruin is content to sink down and become part of its landscape or some other construction, without penetrating into monumental memory.

But sleep is not metamorphosis. At the very most it could be understood as an endomorphosis, as the internal formation or the formation of an interiority where the interior, sealed, seemed wholly projected into the intentions and extensions of wakeful existence. Internal formation, but without a transformation of being. Temporary endomorphosis forever suspended on the limits of form itself, formation of an amorphous, hard-to-identify substance whose most common and well-defined aspect is precisely none other than that of the fall, of sagging and unfastening: the prostrate posture of the god Morpheus.

2

I'm Falling Asleep

By falling asleep, I fall inside myself: from my exhaustion, from my boredom, from my exhausted pleasure or from my exhausting pain. I fall inside my own satiety as well as my own vacuity: I myself become the abyss and the plunge, the density of deep water and the descent of the drowned body sinking backward. I fall to where I am no longer separated from the world by a demarcation that still belongs to me all through my waking state and that I myself am, just as I am my skin and all my sense organs. I pass that line of distinction, I slip entire into the innermost and outermost part of myself, erasing the division between these two putative regions.

    I sleep and this *I* that sleeps can no more say it sleeps than it could say that it is dead. So it is another who sleeps in my place. But so exactly, so perfectly in this, my own place, that he occupies it wholly without overlooking or overflowing even the slightest portion. It is not a part of me, or an aspect, or a function that is sleeping. It is that entire other who I am as soon as I am removed from all aspects of me and from all my functions except the function of sleeping, which perhaps is not a function, or else functions only to suspend all functioning.

Some will say it's a matter of a vegetative functioning. I vegetate, I become a vegetative self, almost vegetable: rooted in its place, only traversed by the slow processes of respiration and other metabolic processes with which organs that take their ease in the relaxation of sleep are occupied. I peacefully and very effectively digest, without any nervous perturbation. A surprising misinterpretation has taken the ancient saying "he who sleeps, eats" [*qui dort dîne*] and drawn from it the maxim that he who sleeps nourishes himself in some way. Originally, it was meant to inform the traveler that if he wanted to sleep at the inn, he would also have to take and pay for his dinner there, instead of unpacking provisions he'd brought for the road.

But the diversion of meaning is not without wisdom: he who sleeps does in fact nourish himself in a way. He who sleeps does not feed on anything that comes to him from without. Like animals that practice hibernation, the sleeper feeds on his reserves. He digests himself, in a way. With its own substance, night also is part of his food. Not the night that surrounds him and that can at times be replaced by day, if the sleeper rests in the middle of the day, but that night he causes to descend from himself into himself, night of the lowered eyelids, even, in extreme circumstances, the night fallen on eyes wide open. Fallen "on" but coming from within, coming from a nightfall inside the sleeper.

I'M FALLING ASLEEP

I now belong only to myself, having fallen into myself and mingled with that night where everything becomes indistinct to me but more than anything myself. I mean: everything becomes more than anything myself, everything is reabsorbed into me without allowing me to distinguish me from anything. But I also mean: more than anything, I myself become indistinct. I no longer properly distinguish myself from the world or from others, from my own body or from my mind, either. For I can no longer hold anything as an object, as a perception or a thought, without this very thing making itself felt as being *at the same time* myself and something other than myself. A simultaneity of what is one's own and not one's own occurs as this distinction falls away.

There is simultaneity only in the realm of sleep. It is the great present, the co-presence of all compossibilities, even incompatible ones. Removed from the bustle of time, from the obsessions of past and future, of arising and passing away,[3] I coincide with the world. *I* am reduced to my own indistinctness, which, however, still experiences itself as an "I" that goes along with its visions without, however, distinguishing itself from them.

This other fall—the fall of distinctions—is added to the first one and gives it its real coherence: I fall asleep,[4] that is to say, "I" fall, "I" no longer exist, or else "I" "exist" only in that effacement of my own distinction. In my own eyes, which no longer look at anything, which are turned toward themselves and toward the black spot inside them, "I" no longer distinguish "myself." If I dream of actions and words of which I am the subject, it is always in such a way that this subjectivity does not distinguish itself or distinguishes itself poorly, *at the same time*, from what it sees, hears, and perceives in general. Such is, in fact, the quite singular awareness of the dream that this awareness thinks itself, and does not think itself as awareness of a world contrasted with it as the waking world is. At every instant the dreamer thinks he is in the waking world and knows he is in the dream world, whose simultaneities, compossibilities, confusions do not escape him but also do not surprise him enough to make him emerge from the dream. We could say that the dream knows it is unaware and that through it, sleep itself knows itself as such and wants to be thus: its fall is not a loss of consciousness but the conscious plunge of consciousness into unconsciousness, which it allows to rise up in itself as it sinks down into it. The truth of this immersion overflows and carries away any sort of analysis.

* * *

Among the thousand sons of Hypnos, Morpheus is identified as the one who is clever at donning the shape and features of mortals, unlike those who imitate animals, plants, or other species of things. Thus Morpheus can, setting aside his dark plumage, come down to Alcyone's bed and in a dream make her recognize Ceyx, her vanished husband. Alcyone moves her arms as she sleeps and wants to embrace Ceyx, but it's air she embraces. Awake, she runs to the shore and sees the body of her vanished beloved on the waves. She leaps toward him from the top of the jetty, for wings have sprouted on her and now she can fly. She wraps her wings around the frigid body and with her beak seeks out and strokes his mouth. The gods change Ceyx in turn into a bird and the pair of kingfishers find on the waves their first love and the floating nest of their marriage.

Such is Morpheus, such is the virtue of his kiss. Anamorphosis of the real form, metamorphosis of life into death and again into life, into life stolen, into life flown away and suspended on the waves, into wet life, into love streaming in the hollow of waves. Morpheus transforms the pure matter of sleep into form. He gives shape and flight to the shapeless and to the fall. His metamorphosis contains the very mystery of sleep: the outline of a fluidity, the look, sign, and gesture of evanescence with the charm and virtue of presence.

3

Self from Absence to Self

What a self it is that allows itself to be discovered! Fallen from the supposed heights of vigilant consciousness, from surveillance and control, from projection and differentiation, here is a self given over to its most intimate motion: that of the return into self. What, in fact, is "self" if not "to oneself," "for oneself"? Self relates to self and returns to itself to be what it is: "self." "I" do not make a self, for "I" do not return: *I*, on the contrary, escape, either by addressing the world or by withdrawing from it, but only in order to lose its isolated distinction of "I" (which is also that of "you" singular or any entanglement in an "us" or a "you" plural). I fall asleep and at the same time I vanish as "I."

I fall into myself and myself falls into self. It is no longer me, it is oneself, which does nothing but return to self. We say, in French, that someone who regains consciousness after fainting "comes back to himself [*revient à soi*]." But actually, he comes back to the distinction of "I" and "you," he comes back to setting himself apart from the world. When he fainted, he was only self, self immediately brought to itself, so that this very bringing back, this return from self to self, is annulled as a return, since it serves in brief as the shortcut, or even the short-circuit, of any kind of "return."

The difference, though, stems from the fact that fainting is done without the consent of the "I," which, by contrast, usually assents to sleep and desires it. It probably has to conclude by sinking into it, even losing its consent, by becoming nothing else but its own fall, until it consists precisely in no longer being "its own" but in rejoining the indistinct space where we all sleep like one another—neither more nor less, though, than we wake up like each other, so long as it's only a matter of considering "wakefulness" as such.

No longer being one's own, no longer properly being in relation to the self-ness of oneself, but more deeply and more obscurely being in self in such a way that the question of "one's own" tends to disappear (Am I really me? Am I actually what I am, what I have to be?) comes back to sleeping, for it demands the dissipation of questioning and the anxiety that animates it. "Who am I?" disintegrates in the fall of sleep, for this fall carries me toward the absence of questions, toward the unconditional and indubitable affirmation—alien to any system of doubt, to any condition of identification—of a being-in-self [*être-à-soi*] that tolerates no unpacking, no analysis of its structure. It is not responsible for some problematic of "relation to self" [*rapport à soi*] or of "presence to self" [*présence à soi*]: neither relation nor presence have to be asserted here. Nor

SELF FROM ABSENCE TO SELF

can the form or general logic of "to," of "be to," be asserted: the "to" in sleep has yielded to "in." It is in the self the sleeper is, as *in self* as the Kantian *thing* can be, that is the being-there, posited, the very position independent of all appearance and all appearing.

The sleeping *self* does not appear: it is not phenomenalized, and if it dreams of itself, that is, as I have said, according to an appearing that leaves no room for a distinction between being and appearing. Sleep does not authorize the analysis of any form of appearance whatsoever, since it shows itself to itself as this appearance that appears only as non-appearing, as returning all appearing on itself and in itself, allowing the waking phenomenologist approaching the bed to perceive nothing but the appearance of its disappearance, the attestation of its retreat.

There is no phenomenology of sleep, for it shows of itself only its disappearance, its burrowing and its concealment. But by concealing itself, it brings, on the other hand, the possibility, further and stronger than any phenomenality, of a deposition of intentions and aims as well as the fulfillment of sense. Sense, here, neither fulfills nor enlightens. It overflows and obscures signification, it makes sense only of sensing oneself no longer appearing.

In this non-appearing, one single thing shows itself. But it does not show itself to others, and in this precise sense it does not appear. It shows itself to itself and, even better, in accordance with the distinction posited, it shows itself *in* itself, it appears to itself in that minute and intimate interstice between self and self, there where self is self. That is why its philosophical expression is indeed this "I am," this *ego sum* that Descartes does not doubt is independent of whether or not I sleep and of whether or not everything I perceive is on the order of dream.

"I am," however, heard murmured by the unconsciousness of a dreamer, testifies less to an "I" strictly conceived than to a "self" simply withdrawn into self, out of reach of any questioning and of any representation. Murmured by unconsciousness, "I am" becomes unintelligible; it is a kind of grunt or sigh that escapes from barely parted lips. It is a preverbal stream that deposits on the pillow a barely visible trace, as if a little saliva had leaked out of that sleeping mouth.

The man or woman whose mouth thus mumbles a confused attestation of existence is no longer "I" and is not truly "self": but beyond the two, or simply set apart, indifferent to any kind of ipseity; he or she is in self in the sense of the *thing in itself* that Kant made famous, not without risking more than one misunderstanding. The thing in itself is nothing other than the thing itself, but withdrawn from any relation with a subject of its perception or with an agent of its manipulation. The thing, isolated from all manifestation, from all phenomenality, the sleeping thing at rest, sheltered from knowledge, techniques, and arts of all kinds, exempt from judgments and prospects. The thing not measured, not measurable, the thing concentrated in its indeterminate and non-appearing thingness.

> Sleep is the state where the soul is plunged into its undifferentiated unity—waking, on the other hand, is the state in which the soul has entered into opposition to this simple unity.[5]

The sleeping self is the self of the thing in itself: a self that cannot even distinguish *itself* from what is not "self," a self without self, in a way, but that finds or touches in this being-without-self its most genuine autonomous existence. Further, this existence should rightly be called absolute: *ab-solutum*, it is detachment from everything, it is that from which every link, every relation, every connection or composition, has been dissolved and excluded. It is that which essentially comes undone, detaches itself and releases itself even from any relation with its own detachment. The thing in itself knows nothing about other things, and everything that appears to it or makes itself felt to it comes only from itself, comes to it in self from self, without any distance to travel, without any performance to present.

There is no representation, there is barely presentation, barely presence. The presence of the sleeper is the presence of an absence, the thing in itself is a thing of no-thing. Mass, though, which is massive, massed, rolled, curled around this self that exists by insisting on a nonexistence. Not, however, pushed or driven back into a stupefaction: on the contrary, rapt in fervor, in an adoration of the world where it opens its strange peace.

4

Equal World

Everything is equal to itself and to the rest of the world. Everything reverts to the general equivalence in which one sleeper is worth as much as any other sleeper and every sleep is worth all the others, however it may appear. For sleeping "well" or "badly" comes down merely to sleeping more or less, in a more or less continuous, or more or less perturbed fashion. Interruptions and perturbations, including those that arise sometimes from within sleep itself, like those nightmares that wake us up in anxiety and sweat—these accidents of sleep do not belong to it.

Sleep itself knows only equality, the measure common to all, which allows no differences or disparities. All sleepers fall into the same, identical and uniform sleep. This consists precisely in not differentiating. That is why night suits it, along with darkness, and especially silence. Likewise, too, a necessary apathy—passions, sorrows, and joys must be asleep, desire must rest too, and even contact, or the smell of the bed, of its sheets, and of the companion, if there is one, with whom one sleeps.

Everyone sleeps in the equality of the same sleep—all the living—and that is why it might seem strange to assert that sleeping together is such a high-risk undertaking. But we are well aware of this, and for us, at least, whose culture has forgotten the way our ancestors slept together collectively, sleeping together evokes nothing less than what we call in the crudest way (but why crude? except because we have thus twisted the sense of words, at least in the French language) "going to bed together."

Sleeping together opens up nothing less than the possibility of penetrating into the most intimate part of the other, namely, precisely into his or her sleep. The happy, languid sleep of lovers who sink down together prolongs their loving spasm into a long suspense, into a pause held at the limits of the dissolution and disappearance of their very harmony: intermingled, their bodies insidiously disentangle, however intertwined they can sometimes remain until the end of sleep, until the instant joy returns to them as renewed for having been forgotten, eclipsed during the time of their sleep, where their agile bodies surface again after having been drowned at the bottom of the waters they themselves poured out.

> The separation, comma [*virgule*], between *l'émoi*, *et moi*, excitement, and I, on waking [*au reveil*], is equal to decollating [*décoller*] (detachment of the neck [*cou*] and of glue [*la colle*]), and decollation to a sublimating idealization that relieves what is detached. Indecision,

oscillation, the trembling vibration where ideality is announced, these are always called shuddering, quivering, and so on. "That kind of shudder also exalted my happiness, for it made our trembling kiss seem to take wing [*décoller*], to be idealized. . . . that he had been on the alert all the time and that, during the embrace, he had not been roused [*ému*], for on hearing the noise he would have had slight [*légère*] difficulty, despite his quick reflexes, in shaking off the excitement, and I [*l'émoi, et moi*], who was glued to him, would have detected that slight twinge, that decollation of a subtle glue [*glu*]" (*Miracle of the Rose*).[6]

But this forgetting itself pertains to the rapture [*jouissance*] in which there is nothing to take or keep, nothing to win or save: everything, on the contrary, to let go. Sleep enjoys prolonging the pleasure whose evaporation and exhaustion it consumes. It grants full rights to the power of extinction that ardor bears within it: it provides it, not with the easing that is supposed to follow tension, but with the very subtle conversion of tension into the intensity of relaxation that physics calls inertia and that keeps a body in momentum so long as no friction of surrounding matter comes to oppose the pursuit of its trajectory.

Sleeping together comes down to sharing an inertia, an equal force that maintains the two bodies together, drifting like two narrow boats moving off to the same open sea, toward the same horizon always concealed afresh in mists whose indistinctness does not let dawn be distinguished from dusk, or sunset from sunrise.

* * *

For it is in effect the great equal sleep of the whole Earth that those who sleep together share. In their "together" is refracted the entirety of all sleepers: animals, plants, rivers, seas, sands, stars set in their crystalline spheres of ether, and ether itself, which has fallen asleep. But the truth of ether—whether it exists or whether it doesn't exist, as we have known it since Michelson and Morley—is that it falls asleep and that it puts to sleep our planetary system with it. It is the great sleep, the great night of the world that surrounds us, toward which we drift irresistibly in an infinite expansion.

For there to be night, though, there must be day. Day introduces night as its own difference and as the alternation by which alone there can be *day*: meaning both daylight and a period of time. Twofold scansion, twofold alternation, of light and darkness, of the unity of time that succeeds itself. Twofold rhythm, solar and lunar, waking and sleeping. *Fiat lux*—and there is the first day, wholly made up of its sole brilliance of day, but there at the same time is time itself, the rhythmic balance of days and nights. The first day of the world, the first night, the first difference. Equal to itself, this beat turns every day and all the days that God makes—as we used to say back in the days of God—into succession itself, the successiveness of time, which passes equal to itself in its obstinate cadence.

This equality to itself is distributed according to the rhythmic distinction between the inequality of day and the equality of night. Day by itself is unequal, singular, just as the primal *lux* was and is always nothing other than difference itself, the division of the primeval indistinctness of a

EQUAL WORLD

chaos, a *khōra*, a magma, an upwelling watertable. Day is always another day, it is, in general, the other of the same. Tomorrow is another day, that is to say, again a day and a different day. The passage to this other is created by the equality of night. All nights are equal. All equally suspend the time of difference, the time of differentiations of all kinds, like that of speech, of food, of combat, of travel, of thought.

Nights can indeed differ among themselves—contrast a night of insomnia to a night sealed under leaden sleep. Nights can offer the contrasts of lamps lit and fires extinguished, of nighttime celebrations and dozing households: but it is night nonetheless, night always begun anew. Days can indeed, for their part, resemble each other in the most repetitive monotony, in the *quotidian* whose name signifies one-day-always-like-another, but they still contrast with each other as much as one light differs from another and one shadow from another.

Night erases the relationship of light with shadow. Night obstinately brings indifference back into the different; it finds the previous world, the magma, the chaos, the *khōra*, equality posed on itself, the bodies of lovers at the bottom of the sea, the equivalence of hours no longer recorded by the unequal shadow of any sundial and measured only by the constant and arbitrary unit of the falling drop of water, or else the transition of an atom of caesium 133 from state A to state B.

* * *

THE FALL OF SLEEP

Sleep is engendered by night. Without night it would have no place to exist, and living beings would be organized in such a way that they could bustle about in a perpetual day without wearing out. That, incidentally, is why occupying night, invading it by work, is the obsession of systems of production. Night shifts are set up; artificial lighting is contrived; and night, suspense, the dwindling of daylight are all chased away. The rhythm of the unequal and the equal is suppressed; everything is equalized in the constantly renewed inequality of *input* and *output*, the measured values of pressure, tension, stocking and destocking, charge and discharge.

But night, for its part, night, which continues to persist around factories and electrified offices, allows no measure other than itself. It wraps up the day and conceals it. It puts it in reserve for the other day that awaits it and that it awaits, but it invests space and time with this waiting. It arranges the positions, disarms the systems of activation, and disconnects networks, and it is in the indistinctness thus created that this great dark cloud comes in which everything is enveloped and withdrawn: this cloud called "night," sweet Night, who walks with an imperceptible rustle of her long, starry skirts.

Sleep comes to meet her; it recognizes her as its law and its element: it follows close behind her, it lets itself be dragged into its shift of inertia, it espouses her cause, her insistent demand for equality. Sleep is the recognition of night: it greets her and pays homage to her. It lets itself be adopted by her. It melts into her. Sleep becomes night itself. Sleep itself becomes the return to the immemorial world, to the world from beyond the world, to the world of obscure gods who utter no creative word.

5

"To sleep, perchance to dream, ay, there's the rub..."

The sleeping person closes his eyes so he can open them to night. Inside himself, beneath the eyelids that sink with sleep and that were already there, throughout the whole day, solely that there might be evoked, lowering their awnings at times, the always possible imminence of a night in broad daylight, the possibility, if not the necessity, of escaping the solicitations of wakefulness, what he sees is nothing other than night itself. For night—through a major difference from day—is no more external than it is internal. Day is wholly outside; day is before our eyes, at the tip of our hands and feet, on our tongue, and in the porches of our ears. Night identifies outside with inside; the eye sees in it the underside of things, the back of the eyelids, the invisible layer of the other side of things, the underpinnings, crypts, skins turned inside out. It is the world of *substance*, that which exists underneath and itself exists on nothing else. That which is not *accident* or *attribute*, that is, it comes to nothing and refers or applies to nothing, except to itself:

that which is entirely its own, belonging to no other subject or support, to no authority of validation or justification.

Night reigns unjustified and sleep espouses this abandonment of justification, its position offside and off-camera. More precisely: it might have been conceivable for living beings not to sleep at night, not to sleep at all, or else to reverse the nycthemeral rhythm, as some of them do, bats, vampires, and eagle owls. But night's case had to be heard. Besides, at the very first, the one who uttered *Fiat lux* must somewhere have taken part in sleep. God must have slept, on the first night, for without that he could not next day have differentiated the rest of his work. He slept every night and he still sleeps upon all those nights that separate all the days he continues to make, or that continue to make themselves without him.

Sleep is divine for this reason, and the most uniquely divine thing revealed in it is the suspense of creative speech. No "*Let there be this!*" is uttered, no commandment to make something come to be. There is a silent obedience to the difference of the being: to this "nothing," to this "no thing," to this *ex nihilo* that light first drove back to the heart of darkness in the movement by which it sprang from it. Light shaped nothing as darkness: it configured it as figureless, as the thing removed from all things.

What the sleeper sees is this eclipsed thing. He sees the eclipse itself: not the fiery ring around it, but the perfectly dark heart of the eclipse of being. But this darkness is not an invisibility: on the contrary, it offers the full visibility of what, in front of me—that *in front* where every image comes to be imaged, every color to shimmer, every outline traced—

"TO SLEEP, PERCHANCE TO DREAM..."

there is no more "in front" and everything is made equivalent to "in back" or to "nowhere." There is no share of the visible, consequently there is no invisible either. There is no division or partition. Everything that could come from outside or escape to it, all the supposed "messages" and any thoughts, whether they be of the eye or the ear, the nose, the mouth or the skin, the nerves, the viscera, the neuron chains, muscles and tendons, wills or imaginations, desires or sufferings, all thoughts without exception do not disappear—far from it!—but come to play freely, indistinctly distinct, in the expanse of nowhere, in the null part of this eclipsed world gathered in this point of sleeping equality.

Sometimes, dream occurs. "Perchance," as Hamlet says—he whose entire life and thinking are in a way devoted to nothing but sleep, to its shadow as well as to its shade [*à sa tombée comme à sa tombe*]. *Perchance* to dream, that is to say, perchance something of night passing into day, by chance, by misfortune or by capricious luck. All of a sudden, awakening finds close to it a scrap left over from sleep. Something was brought back from nothing, and in effect it is a configuration of nothing: scenes often colorful, with all kinds of tones, but whose dense coherency becomes blurred and quickly breaks apart in the acidity of day, all the more so in the fantasies or phantasms of interpretation that, in the end, regularly and necessarily loses itself in the depths of that *navel of the dream* Freud speaks of to emphasize that everything here occurs before birth, before any distinction and any separation, any discernment of person or sense.

Dream like waking, similar to it, and dream as waking. Dream in place of waking. The daydream already shapes sleep in broad daylight, sleep in the midst of waking. The wakefulness of waking lets itself go. Fragile reverie bleaches the real and paints over it, washed out, without depth, in thin, contiguous layers, a somnolent world into which the dreamer sinks and is lost. When it has reached the place where neither the slightest solidity nor the least density of any kind of outside persists, dream can arise. Or rather, it can spread like a lazy painting slowly worked onto the black canvas displayed at the bottom of sleep: a hazy or Fauvist painting, pointillist or hyperrealist, broad washes and negligent brushstrokes, motionless in movement, the image shaking; we guess the shot was taken using an array of lenses too complicated for its machinery to be dismantled, but whose presence we sense is quite close, a copper and ebony apparatus loaded with enlarging and distorting lenses, magnifying glasses and beveled mirrors, a cinematographic device without motor but endowed with zoom lenses and dollies and booms stacked onto each other and moving effortlessly, with no hint of the space in which they move. This mobility penetrates into the barely formed image and goes through it like a pebble through the surface of a pond, making concentric waves in which there tremble repeated modulations of the central motif, whose outline is at the same time lost and recomposed suddenly elsewhere, unrecognizable, substituted and despite everything entirely superimposed on the motif it both replaces and repeats, tracing an indecipherable figure against the violent ambivalence from which the dreamer's mind feels projected with the insistency of certainty bogged down in doubt. Already he no longer knows if he has lost the thread or never even started to grasp its slightest appearance; he realizes that everything is unrealized, withdrawing the thing from him as it presses its weight and affects him

"TO SLEEP, PERCHANCE TO DREAM . . ."

with its heavy presence, insinuating, threatening even, and he almost cries out, but his very cry cannot cry out: the sound seems cut off, stifled even before being fully formed in the back of his throat as, in front of him, on the screen, on the variegated phantasmagoric diorama, familiar faces can be recognized, complicated by bizarre features, ordinary situations made solemn, and erotic movements crushed against skin imbued with a precise, keen, inimitable sensation, which most exactly imitates the pattern and voice of an ancient desire, a boldness long repressed whose antennae in this very place, as it rushes forward, the fine thread of the dream entraps in the way a spider holds prisoner the antennae of an insect caught in its web. And that is how the web, the canvas [*toile*] painted and languidly moving on this carnival stage, is resolved into a network of silvery filaments on which a drop of dew or a tear trembles, whose imminent fall will destroy the web and startle the spider, whose feet finally sink into the bottom of the dreaming eyes, down to the affected retina, on which soon will alight the suddenly recognized sparkle of awakening, that waking whose place will have been so well, so truly, so intimately, and so irreversibly filled that it is for a time impossible for the dreamer not to wonder in his soul and consciousness whether it was there, whether it's still now and precisely there, in front of him in the night that yet again reveals to him its vibrant blackness, the real and indisputable truth that ought to make him doubt the possibly utterly false meaning of his situation, like a sleeper awakened by the fall of his own dream further into the sleep that now escapes him. (At dawn, the animal laps up the juice of nocturnal flowers.)

THE FALL OF SLEEP

This time of wondering whether I'm dreaming or waking is the time most suited for an awareness that knows itself without knowing what it knows by knowing itself thus. It knows quite well it is awareness, but it does not know what it is or is not aware of, and, in the end, it does not know what "awareness" means and what correlation of object or intention an awareness is entitled to ensure: it only knows that it wonders if it's night all round it or if the sun has risen, so that it can assure itself of only one thing, namely, that in the depths of its being or its condition is the deepest night, the black night in which it itself is the vigorous sleepwalker. Are we permitted to say, as Freud supposes, that sleep lowers our defenses? Shouldn't we, rather, esteem this considerable increase of our world as equal to the night of an outside-the-world within which we come to float like astronauts who work in space wearing those enormous spacesuits that make their gestures look clumsy and their thoughts hazy? But beneath their blurry appearance, astronauts carry out precise maneuvers and delicate operations. Like the maneuvers, operations, conducts, techniques, and arts deployed in the broad spaces of sleep.

*   *   *

—the innocent sleep,
Sleep that knits up the ravel'd sleave of care,
The death of each day's life, sore labor's bath,
Balm of hurt minds, great nature's second course,
Chief nourisher in life's feast—[7]

6

Lullaby

> Let us sleep, not knowing each other. Breast against breast,
> Breath intermingled, hand in hand dreamless.
> —Yves Bonnefoy, "Une pierre," in *Les Planches courbes*

Still, we have to put ourselves to sleep [*s'être endormi*]. But this reflexive verb leads to an illusion. No one puts himself to sleep: sleep comes from elsewhere. It falls onto us, it makes us fall into it. So we have to have been put to sleep. We have to have been put to sleep by sleep itself—by the sleep of exhaustion or the sleep of pleasure, by the sleep of boredom—or else by some access road to its realm.

What leads to sleep has the shape of rhythm, of regularity and repetition. It is a matter of nothing but mimicry, since sleep itself is rhythm, regularity and repetition. Sleeping does not consist of a process like that of walking, eating, or thinking. The only processes that belong to sleep are those of respiration and circulation. They themselves are put to rest, they find a slower cadence there, a deeper amplitude scarcely differentiated moment by moment. When it goes to sleep, the body is rocked to the rhythm of its heart and lungs.

Cultures have developed a great store of ways to lull, from rocking a child on its mother's back on her way to the washhouse or the well down to all manner of cradles and cribs—operated by foot or by hand, hanging from cords, mounted on springs, floating on water—rocking the child in one's arms or else riding on the back of a donkey or camel, in a car or else in those strapped-on carriers that make young fathers look like a sort of technological marsupial, and don't forget music boxes or those languid mobiles adrift over infant beds.

But whatever one's age, no one enters sleep without some sort of lullaby. No one can do without being led along by a cadence one does not even perceive, since it is precisely the cadence of absence that penetrates presence, sometimes in one single movement—in one single push that suddenly sends the present floating alongside itself—sometimes at several times—in several successive waves, like a tide licking the sand and impregnating it a little further each time, depositing flakes of sleepy foam. Rocking movements put us to sleep because sleep in its essence is itself a rocking, not a stable, motionless state. *Lullaby*: one charms, one enchants, one puts mistrust to sleep before putting wakefulness itself to sleep, one gently guides to nowhere—*swing low, sweet chariot, comin' for to carry me home*.

Just as night represents a time of cosmic rhythm and sleep a time of biological rhythm, so also does sleep compose in itself the rhythm in which its profound nature is

LULLABY

reflected. Rocking is a matter of high and low and of right and left, of the great symmetries, asymmetries, and alternations that govern crystals, tides, seasons, the cycles of planets and their satellites, exchanges of oxygen and carbon dioxide, captures and releases, assimilations and evacuations, nervous systems, attractions and repulsions between metals, between fauna and flora, between sexes, between stellar masses, black holes, quarks, and infinitesimal jets of dust . . . It is a matter, to conclude or rather to begin, of the initial beat between something and nothing, between the world and the void, which also means between the world and itself.

It is a matter of the space in between, without which no reality can take place and without which, accordingly, no reality is real without a connection to some other reality from which it is separated by the interval that distinguishes them and that links them to each other according to the very pulsation of their common nonorigin [*inorigine*]—since in fact nothing makes or marks origin, nothing but the spacing and balancing of *nihil* among things, beings, substances or subjects, positions, places, times. Nothing but the swaying of the world makes the cradle or rather cradling within which everything awakens—awakening to sleep as well as to waking, awakening to self as well as to throbbing and rocking in general.

Cadence, caress, pendulum motion, to-and-fro of hands, of lips, tongues, and moist genitals, rising and falling of swells, rises and jerks of spasms before return to the long rollers, the deep waves.

Rocking of before the world, rocking of being on nothing, of nothing on nothing, equal balance between nothing and being, being nothing and being something, to be nothing, to be only something, to be some things balancing between themselves, singularly equal different from nothing, differing from almost nothing, from the infinitesimal, immemorial difference that is nothing, truly nothing, but without which nothing would be revealed as different from anything.

Above, below, to the right, to the left, imperceptibly, without any above, or below, or left, or right, just the slim beam of the scales that weigh the thinking of the world, that weigh its justice, its uncompromising equanimity, all those things indistinctly thrown at the same common unworking [*désoeuvrement*] effortlessly making a world, doing nothing, causing to come into the world, making a world come, lighting it, darkening it, covering it with lands and seas, discovering its rocks and sludges, raising and lowering the waters, lifting and toppling mountain peaks, summits, abysses, unfastening moons, rings, atolls, aurora borealises, dawns and dusks, little disks, little puddles of light, little communion wafers swallowed by night, lower down, further below, passing far behind to come back on the other side and to hold anew a dawn suspended, gray, indistinct and precise in the outline of a new horizon, a new frontier between nowhere and somewhere, between never and now, drafting of sketches on the background of erased traces, rough drafts resumed, retouches, approaches, eternal returns of the same lines, refrain, *Morgen früh, wenn Gott will, wirst du wieder erweckt.*

Tomorrow morning, God willing, you will awake again: sleep my child, sleep my soul, sleep my world, sleep

LULLABY

my love, sleep my little one, the child will sleep soon, already he's sleeping, look, he goes to sleep with the first night of the world, the divine child who plays with the dice of the universe and of all its centuries, he sleeps with every night that rocks anew, tirelessly, the repetition of the first, of the initial nocturnal lullaby where the first day fell asleep with the first sleep.

7

The Soul That Never Sleeps

Never, however, never does the soul sleep. That absenting of self in self is unknown to it. Absence belongs to the body and to the mind; it is foreign to the soul. In sleep, the mind abandons itself to the body and disperses its location through it, dissolves its concentration into that soft, almost disjointed expanse. The body, for its part, abandons itself paradoxically to the very location of the mind: it is no longer actually exposed in space but implicitly or virtually withdrawn into a nonplace where it anaesthetizes itself and separates itself from the world. The person who sleeps is a mental body or a bodily mind, one lost in the other, and in both cases, in both aspects, a subject extravasated, aspirated, *ex-posed* or *ex-isting* in the strongest and most problematic senses of these words. In this the sleeper is always twofold. He, she is himself, herself, and another. Their very sex is undecided then more deeply than it is ever so in other conditions, for sleep seduces itself and takes pleasure in itself—which is not an "itself."

THE FALL OF SLEEP

But the soul animates sleep as well as waking. The soul is both sleeping and vigilant, and for that very reason it does not sleep. Nor is it awakened: in waking it is that which ceaselessly dozes, in sleeping it is that which wakes and watches—from all quarters, every time, it is that which, giving form and tonality to a presence, adheres to the edges, to the outlines. Not, indeed, like a skipper in his ship, but spread throughout the entire expanse of the body and mingled with it so that simultaneously at every point it is like a signal, like a lantern, like a lookout on top of a tall mast or like a sated seagull on the taffrail. It is like a Saint Elmo's fire or like a brilliant moonbeam on copper, or like a message thrown into the sea, or else like a radio antenna capturing a call for help from another boat set adrift by its failing engines, or like the glint of the sun on the lenses of the binoculars in which the image appears of a shabby old tub loaded with boat people who are dying, falling from misery and fear, falling, fallen into a sleep that no longer sleeps, into a dreary lethargy of woe.

* * *

The soul models and modulates the form of the sleeper as well as that of the waker: it receives and emits for both of them the signals from the rest of the world but also signals from the other, from the sleeper huddled inside the waker, from the waker circling inside the sleeper. It keeps the one who wakes from abandoning himself to all the slings and arrows of the day; it blinks his eyelids and makes him share the beneficial forgetfulness so necessary to the pursuit of works and days. It maintains the one

THE SOUL THAT NEVER SLEEPS

who sleeps in a state that perceives emergency signals and ruminates over his most intimate thoughts.

It is not insomniac, this soul: quite the contrary, it is indeed the soul that sleeps with the sleep of the sleeper and that wakes with the wakefulness of the one awake. It is the soul that watches in the midst of sleep and that sleeps only in waking. It is the watch itself that divides between night and day, between vigilant watchfulness and somnolent watchfulness. It itself is the rhythm, it is the gently dancing shadow that keeps watch all the time over the possibility of alternation and rocking, over this turn-by-turn without which we would be either dead or else would be living beings standing stiff in their heroic posture, like that Socrates able to spend the whole night standing up: vigilance itself, the idea bright without shadow, and also without music.

But we have to keep watch. We have to keep watch when even the soul would like to go to sleep. In the end it has to stop watching over sleep.

Ambulances tear through the night, and cannons, and rocket launchings, children crying, tanks rumbling, rending pains in the chest, in the bellies of the cancerous or the wounded, harsh light of lamps that one cannot or will not turn off, obsessive thoughts, torments, remorse, feverish anticipations, fears—fears more than anything else, fears of everything.

Sleep presupposes the fear of night has been conquered—but night is the wilderness of fears. The figures that day arranges for recognition rise up again from the darkness disguised in evil masks, the thoughts we know how to manage carefully burst into anxieties, suffocations,

THE FALL OF SLEEP

aporias that close over and over onto themselves as long as day has not dissolved them. Night engenders terror, obsession, ravage, and panic. It is not a matter of insomnia, which is a wandering from sleep itself, its transformation into a wakefulness deprived of day, into a glowing nightlight whose gleam maintains the agitation of the soul with a clear awareness of sleep usurped, split open, transformed into its twofold awakening. On the contrary, it is a matter of the world in which it is impossible to sleep, of the world in which it is forbidden to sleep because of a process of torture whose effectiveness is not in doubt.

* * *

It is possible that the world today is that way: without sleeping or waking. Sleeping standing up, waking while dozing. Sleepwalking and somnolent. World deprived of rhythm, world that has deprived itself of rhythm, that has stripped away from itself the possibility of seeing its days and its nights correspond to the system of nature or history. Migrating birds at night are thrown off course by the intense halo of light that big cities project into the sky: they are ready to go to sleep anywhere, thinking they have reached sunny climes. World in shambles, out of balance, uneven enough to make sleep itself devastated by unevenness. Sleepers harassed, always on the alert, less fallen asleep than thrown into sleep, precipitated by a numbness from short hours broken by knocking sounds in the head, knocks on the door, blows or gunshots. Sleepers not so much sleeping as knocked out, conquered at night as they were during the day, piled into camps or lying in ditches, in trucks or in skiffs, hunted, chased from their hurried repose. Nights shot through with flashes of fire, of frenzy, of famine. Nights stripped of their very night, uprooted from darkness and shadow, thrown into the harsh light of a nuclear blinding. Sleeps that are nothing but parodies, caricatures of sleeps, heads kept buried beneath muddy water but kept from giving themselves over to the abandon of deep waters.

How to sleep in a world without a lullaby, without a lulling refrain, without a capacity for forgetting, without unconsciousness itself, since Eros and Thanatos patrol everywhere shamelessly, sardonic watchmen armed with whips and cudgels? How to sleep in a world hypnotized by the vision of its own absence of vision of the world, as well as by the inanity of all visions that have dissolved but that always used to promise awakenings, triumphant mornings following splendid evenings in the blaze of which night has been forever discredited?

How to sleep, distraught soul, soul without soul, soul that floats lifeless over the field of battle or muck whose inanity an operating-room lamp garishly exposes?

8

The Knell [Glas] of a Temporary Death

Like death, sleep, and like sleep, death—but without awakening. Without a rhythm of return, without repetition, without a new day, without tomorrow.

Like death, sleep, for the body stretches out alone there, is alone there outstretched. Outstretched alone there, *there*, a here like nowhere. Nowhere else but a weighty body cast down, laid out, left on the ground. Like sleep, death: body deposed.

A sleep, though, that would be its own waking: an immortality raised in death through this waking, stuck at right angles like the uprising of that which will never rise again. A sleep sleeping elsewhere than in waiting, or else waiting for itself to receive from self the grace of no longer being measured between two wakings, watches, but being solely and without reservation eternally the sleep it is.

Eternal rest: Dormition of the Virgin or of the Seven Sleepers of Ephesus, death that happens in sleep with the

THE FALL OF SLEEP

help of its inattention, even its noninterest. Sleep that occurs to death and makes it like unto it: Rimbaud's sleeper in the valley, who has two red holes in his right side. You'd say he was sleeping: yes, you would say so, and the dead man too would say so if he could speak. He would say he is sleeping and that like any sleeper he has joined eternity: the reverse of time.

The reverse, the reversal and annulment of time, not its turning back to duration deprived of rhythm, not its stretching out flat in torpor and in coma. Not death that endures, but death that falls all at once and by falling disappears. Death whose fall raises the *tumbos*, the *tumulus*, the gentle, grave elevation of earth or stone in silent prayer.

One could say that sleep is a temporary death, but one could also say that death is necessarily temporary, for it lasts only as long as time lasts. There where time no longer lasts—*there where*, of course, and not *when*, for no time is given for that, only a place apart from all places, not another place, or a *u-topia*, but the outside-place [*hors-lieu*] of apartness itself, the spacing, openness, the beat of rhythm, in sum—there where time no longer lasts, is immobilized upon itself, that is to say on the passage and the *not* or *pace* or *step* [pas] that it is. It suspends itself on this negation that is its fluid being and that shapes the form of every present and every presence: *already not* [déjà pas] and *not yet* [pas encore]. The form of *not* outlines a hollow, it presses a footprint in the sand of shores that we keep approaching and leaving. A hollow, a hollowing out, an elevation, the immobile and immutable rhythm of the grave and the tomb, the respiration of the death sleep.

THE KNELL OF A TEMPORARY DEATH

Not—says the sleeper as well as the dead man, I am not there. Not there, not now, not here, not thus. Look elsewhere, passersby who observe a moment of silence in front of my deathbed. I have gone to the country of the great sleep, I hear your gentle voices singing "Old Black Joe"[8]—and here I am, I tell you, here I am sleeping in peace near you but hidden as much as it is possible to be from all this time that matters to you and that makes you wait for me some more, wait for me like a revenant or like a revived one when I am already there, there where it's a question of arriving to discern the darkness itself as the sole light and the sole thing to see, like vision itself. There, nowhere, where it's a question of consenting to the outside finally carrying away everything inside. There where the self finally sets the self free.

Not here, not thus, but in oneself finally changed: oneself, no one, in that precious abandon of an immortal sleep where no figure, no attempt to take on an identity fashioned on any model whatsoever, no action or remarkable thought can be substituted for that single Same [*Même*] that feels and experiences being eternal, that is to say necessarily inscribed in Substance, God, or Nature, as its same subject, as the inalienable subject of a presence that will never be awakened except to fall asleep immediately in the intimate fainting that plunges it into self—fallen outside itself.

Tomb of Sleep, says this cemetery—every cemetery—where the graves have no other purpose than to offer the assurance of a stone or leaden sleep, a sleep of earth or ash, a sleep without sleep and without insomnia, without awakening and without intention, a limitless sleep: the infinite brought down to the rhythm of each finite existence. *Tombs*, elevations of the soul sleeping the sleep of the just, a mineral body raised for an imploring mingled with adoring. Eternity: time fallen [*tombé*], redressed, risen, revived.

To deprive someone of a grave, to deprive someone of a tomb and of recognition of the body—even a symbolic, analogical, or hypothetical one—to deprive someone of a place reserved for nowhere, to take away even the possibility of a vestige of a passerby's step [*pas*], we know that that is depriving both the dead and the mourners of sleep. The funeral ritual represents something else besides an act of conjuration or compensation. It does not put to sleep the wounded sensibility of the survivors, but it procures for the dead the sleep that comes back to them; that is why it is necessary for tearful survival. The tomb is the intimacy of the dead person so well sealed that it exposes itself utterly, just as the sleeper gives himself up without any risk of betraying a secret, except for this sleep that is not one.

Nothing secret, all appearances appear without trace on the face of the dead and of the sleeping. It is the same appearance without apparency, since it is without backdrop, without a secret drawer, without a hidden heart. The sleeper in fact puts to sleep his whole heart, as does the one who has left without return: he vows his heart to this stopping of the heart. It is not for nothing that we watch over the dying and the dead: our vigil opens a rhythm between the living and the leaving, it inscribes their departure in counterpoint to our vigilant presence. We watch them leave and we see them left; they fall asleep thus in

THE KNELL OF A TEMPORARY DEATH

our eyes as well as in our arms, as in the tomb into whose depths they will never stop vanishing.

It is this interminable disappearance, which neither oblivion nor the slow wearing away of tombs concludes, that preserves in it the eternal emergence of each person one by one, not just a mummy or a yellowing photograph, not just a carved name that has become illegible, not some resemblance in the face of a vague descendant, not a birthmark, not a custom or a manner of speaking, but finally despite everything each grain, each bud, each drop and each leaf, each twinkling signal of a star or an atom, each piece of dust, as perfectly anonymous as it may be, cannot help but sketch out a strange, unsettling, indecipherable sign, the sign without signification of an inconsistent but insistent complicity with no other analogy than that of a common sleep, shared since unshareable.

Like death, sleep, since it withdraws into itself even the simplicity of presence, but like sleep, death, for what it suppresses it presents again immortal to the world or else as the very world on the eve [*veille*] of no tomorrow—and this way watching [*veillant*] over itself, watchman charged with patrolling the only night.

Now, you say, doesn't thinking fall asleep and give way to fantasies? Don't think it for a second. Though it still remains true—painfully true—that the sleep of reason gives birth to monsters, it is no less true that it is by letting itself be inclined to sleep, to dream, and to the possibility of no longer waking that thought lets itself awaken to the last possible day of its full probity: the first day, the day without day of our holy eternity.

9

The Blind Task of Sleep

Whoever does not know how not to wake up, whoever remains on the lookout in the hollow of sleep, he, she, is stuck with his or her fear. He is afraid of letting go even of his troubles and cares. He wears out his night in stirring them, in ruminating over them like thoughts bogged down in tautology, becoming viscous, creeping, insidious, and venomous. But what he fears above all else is not that the difficulties or dangers that these thoughts display threaten to arise as so many failures and defeats on the following day, what he really fears more than these fears themselves is leaving them far behind him and entering the night. He can work with his fear, but this fear tortures the work in turn and makes it uneasy, as if stifled by itself, oppressive and unbalanced, unequal to his art.

> On the backdrop of my nights God's knowing finger
> Draws an unceasing nightmare with many faces.
> I am afraid of sleep as one fears a huge hole

THE FALL OF SLEEP

> Full of vague horror, leading no one knows where;
> I see only infinity from every window,
> And my spirit, ever haunted with vertigo,
> A numb feeling yearning for nothingness.[9]

But into the night, as into sleep, we do not go with our eyes closed. When our eyes are closed, sleep has already won the sleeper. But the instant just before, when eyelids have slipped over our eyes and they for one more moment have remained seers behind their curtain and through the darkness spread everywhere in what we call the bedroom, that is the vault, the curving dome that seals space from sleep by separating it from the celestial vaults themselves—eyelids, bedroom, "canopy [*ciel de lit*]," sublunary world, world of beneath the lids, of ceilings and sheets, world of beneath, crypt hidden to itself—at that instant the gaze has seen the night into which it was entering. What it saw was nothing but the absence of all vision and all visibility. Even that, it saw. He had to bear this sight all the time it took to fall asleep, and it is possible that this horror, worse than a blinding, penetrated the marrow of his sleep to pursue him there and to prevent him finally from truly, profoundly falling asleep.

Not seeing connects with some possibility of help or hope for sight. We do not see in the darkness, which in a way can be dissipated. But seeing that we see nothing and that there is nothing to see, seeing sight clinging to itself as to its sole object, that is like seeing the invisible, surely, but is only like its other side or its negative. To sojourn in just that other side, not to try to discern the invisible, that is the blind task of sleep.[10]

Notes

1. *Tomber de sommeil* is an idiomatic expression meaning "to be ready to drop, to be falling asleep (on one's feet)."—Trans.

2. *Tomber d'ennui*—"to die of boredom, to faint from boredom."—Trans.

3. *Du passé et de l'avenir, du venir et du passer.*

4. *Je tombe de sommeil*, literally "I fall from sleep."—Trans.

5. G. W. F. Hegel, *Hegel's Philosophy of Mind: Part Three of the Encyclopaedia of the Philosophical Sciences*, trans. William Wallace (Oxford: Oxford University Press, 1971), 67. Translation slightly modified.

6. Jacques Derrida, *Glas*, trans. John P. Leavey, Jr., and Richard Rand (Lincoln: University of Nebraska Press, 1986), 132.

7. Shakespeare, *Macbeth*, 2.2.36–39. Nancy quotes these lines by way of the French translation of a German adaptation by Heiner Müller, *Macbeth d'après Shakespeare*: "Sleep that is blameless / Sleep that pacifies the whirlwind of our cares / The death of every day, the bath that cures the oppressed / Balm of the suffering heart, second course of nature / And supreme tribunal of life."—Trans.

8. Stephen Foster's sad song is now a popular Boy Scout song in France as "Le vieux Jo."

9. Baudelaire, "Le Gouffre" ("The Chasm"), *Les fleurs du mal*, my translation.

NOTES

10. In the title of this section, as here, the word translated "task" is *tâche*. There is a play on *tâche* ("task") and *tache* ("spot," as in "blind spot").—Trans.